Searchlight BOOKS™

Do You Dig
Earth Science?

Uncovering

Earth's Crust

Conrad J. Storad

Lerner Publications Company
Minneapolis

For Laurie,
I love exploring the world with you . . .
every day!

Lerner Publications Company
A division of Lerner Publishing Group, Inc.
241 First Avenue North
Minneapolis, MN 55401 U.S.A.

Website address: www.lernerbooks.com

Library of Congress Cataloging-in-Publication Data

Storad, Conrad J.
        Uncovering Earth's crust / by Conrad J. Storad.
            p.   cm — (Searchlight books™—Do you dig earth science?)
        Includes index.
        ISBN 978–1–4677–0020–7 (lib. bdg. : alk. paper)
        1. Earth—Crust—Juvenile literature. 2. Earth—Surface—Juvenile literature. I. Title.
    QE511.S7245 2013
    551.1'3—dc23   2012017604

Manufactured in the United States of America
1 – PC – 12/31/12

Contents

Chapter 1

PLANET PARTS

Take a walk outside. Now look down at your feet. You may be standing on grass or dirt. Or maybe you're standing on concrete or blacktop. You also are standing on Earth's crust.

Earth's crust is always under you. But most of the time you can't see it. Why can't you see the crust?

In most places, the crust is hidden. It may be covered by grass, cornfields, or forests. Or it may be covered by the water in rivers, lakes, or oceans.

IN MANY PLACES, PLANTS AND SOIL COVER EARTH'S CRUST.

A Layer of Rock

But in some places, you can see Earth's crust. Rocky cliffs near the seashore are part of the crust. So are the steep walls of deep canyons.

The crust is a layer of rock that covers our planet. Under the oceans, the crust is about 3 miles (5 kilometers) thick. Under the land, the crust is much thicker. Below your feet, the crust goes down as deep as 40 miles (64 km)! A car driving on a highway takes more than half an hour to go that far.

Part of Earth's crust can be seen in this desert in Arizona.

It might sound as if Earth's crust is really thick. But compared to the whole planet, the crust is actually very thin. Imagine that you could shrink Earth and make it the size of a basketball. Then Earth's crust would be thinner than this book. The tallest mountains would be specks too small to see.

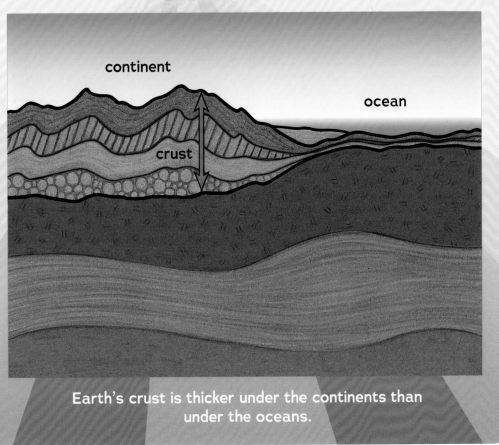

EARTH'S CRUST

continent

ocean

crust

Earth's crust is thicker under the continents than under the oceans.

Continents and Oceans

Earth has huge pieces of land called continents. Most of
Earth is covered by oceans.

THIS IS WHAT EARTH LOOKS
LIKE TO ASTRONAUTS IN SPACE.

But what does Earth look like inside? If you could slice the planet in half, you could see all of its parts. You would see other layers under the crust. Of course, you can't really slice Earth in half. So how do we know about the layers? Geologists tell us. Geologists are scientists who study Earth.

This man is a geologist. He is studying rocks near a volcano.

Studying Earth's Crust

Geologists use special tools to study Earth's parts. They use hammers, picks, and shovels. They also use computers, microscopes, and other tools. Geologists study all of Earth's layers. They study how the layers formed. They also study how the parts of our planet work. Some geologists say Earth's layers are like the parts of a giant hard-boiled egg.

Like Earth, a hard-boiled egg has three main layers. An egg's layers are the shell, the white, and the yolk.

Granite and Basalt

Earth's crust is a thin layer on the outside of the planet. Most of the crust is made of two kinds of rock called granite and basalt. Under the continents, the crust is mostly made of granite. Under the oceans, the crust is mostly made of basalt.

Granite rock comes in many different colors. It is often used to make buildings.

Basalt is usually dark gray. When basalt breaks, the pieces have flat, smooth sides.

A Moving Mantle

Below the crust is a very thick layer of rock. This layer is called the mantle. The mantle is more than 1,800 miles (2,900 km) thick. Most of the rock in the mantle is always moving. But it moves very slowly, kind of like toothpaste being squeezed from a tube.

Magma

The mantle is much hotter than the crust. And the bottom of the mantle is even hotter than the top of the mantle. In some parts of the mantle, rock gets so hot that it melts! Melted rock inside Earth is called magma.

Melted rock glows bright yellow, orange, or red. Its color becomes darker as it cools.

Earth's Core

At Earth's center is another thick layer. This layer is called the core.

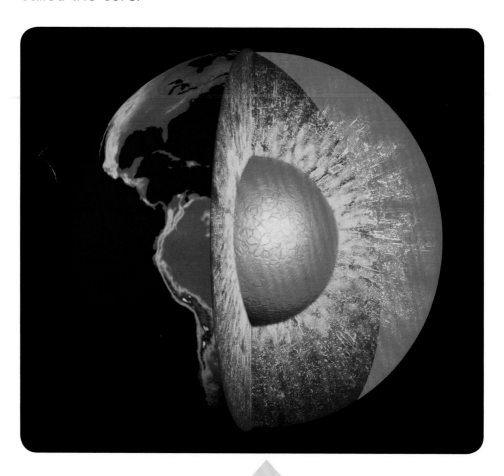

THE CORE IS LOCATED UNDER
THE CRUST AND THE MANTLE.

Earth's core has two parts. The outside part is made of superhot, melted rock. This part is called the outer core. The outer core is more than 1,300 miles (2,092 km) thick. Under the outer core is the inner core. The inner core is made of solid metal. It is more than 1,500 miles (2,414 km) thick.

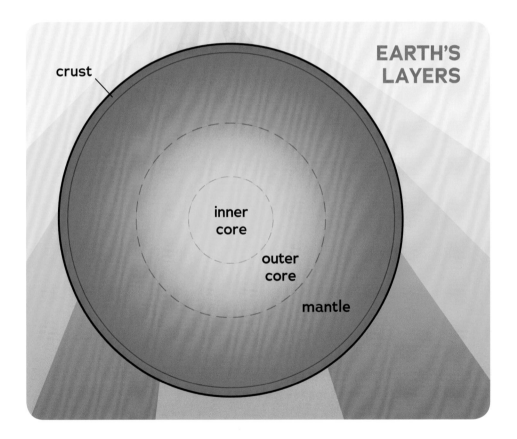

EARTH'S LAYERS

crust

inner core

outer core

mantle

Chapter 2

MOVING PIECES

Earth's crust is not just one piece. Instead, the crust is cracked into lots of big pieces. The pieces are called plates.

Most of Earth's crust is covered up, so you can't see it. If you could see all of Earth's crust, what would it look like?

Geologists say that Earth has seven huge plates and lots of smaller ones. If we could see them, they would look sort of like the pieces of a jigsaw puzzle.

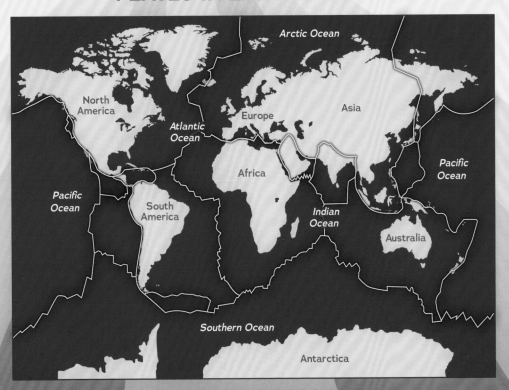

PLATES IN EARTH'S CRUST

Earth's crust is made up of many pieces called plates.
The white lines show the edges of the plates.

Most of these big, rocky plates have both land and water on top of them. But some are covered only by oceans.

Most of Earth's plates have both water and land on them.

Floating Plates

The big plates float on top of the mantle. They do not stay in one place. Instead, they move very slowly across Earth's surface. They can move a long way. But that takes millions of years.

This place in Africa is called the Great Rift Valley. The valley formed because two of Earth's plates are slowly moving away from each other.

The plates carry the continents and the oceans with them as they move. Look at a globe in your classroom. Can you find North America and Europe on the globe? These two continents are on different plates. North America's plate is moving away from Europe's plate. It is not moving very fast, though. It moves only about 1 inch (2.5 centimeters) each year.

North America is one of Earth's continents. This is what North America looks like from space.

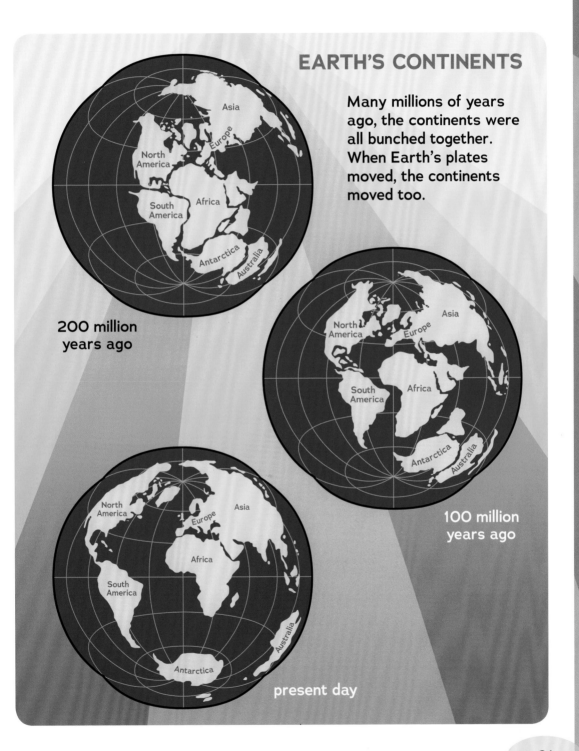

EARTH'S CONTINENTS

Many millions of years ago, the continents were all bunched together. When Earth's plates moved, the continents moved too.

200 million years ago

100 million years ago

present day

Chapter 3

MOUNTAINS, CRACKS, AND HOLES

Sometimes Earth's rocky plates push against one another. It is like a giant wreck in super-slow motion.

Mountains are part of Earth's crust. Why do mountains stick up above the rest of the crust?

Making Mountains

Earth's crust crumples and folds when the big plates smash together. Over millions of years, the folded crust is pushed higher and higher. These big folds in the crust are called mountains.

From space, mountains look like wrinkles in the ground.

Look at the globe again. Look at the Rocky Mountains in North America. Look at the Andes Mountains in South America. Look at the Himalaya Mountains between India and China. These are some of the tallest mountains in the world.

The Rocky Mountains are a long line of mountains. The northern end of the line is in Alaska. The southern end is in Mexico.

Some of the Andes Mountains are so tall that their tops are above the clouds!

The big plates of Earth's crust are crashing together near these mountains. The crust is folding higher and higher. Very, very slowly, the mountains are growing taller.

The Appalachian Mountains are in the eastern United States. These mountains formed a very long time ago.

Faults

Earth's crust may break near the places where the big plates push against each other. Sometimes cracks and holes form in Earth's crust.

Cracks in the crust are called faults. Some faults are deep underground. Other faults can be seen on the surface.

Some of these cracks in the crust are short. But others are very long. The San Andreas Fault in California is one of the most famous cracks in Earth's crust. This fault is more than 700 miles (1,127 km) long.

The San Andreas Fault is a very long crack in Earth's crust.

An Earthquake!

Sometimes pieces of the crust near these giant cracks move. Huge slabs of rock push against each other along a fault. The two slabs try to slide in different directions. The slabs might push against each other for hundreds of years.

AN EARTHQUAKE MADE BIG CRACKS IN THIS ROAD.

Finally, one slab slides past the other slab in a short, powerful movement. The movement of the slabs is called an earthquake. During an earthquake, the ground moves. The ground may shake hundreds of miles away from the fault!

The ground under this building moved during an earthquake. The building broke into pieces.

Volcanoes

Holes also form in Earth's crust. These holes are often close to the edges of the giant plates. Holes in the crust are called volcanoes. Beneath a volcano is a huge space called a magma chamber. It is filled with hot magma, which is melted rock.

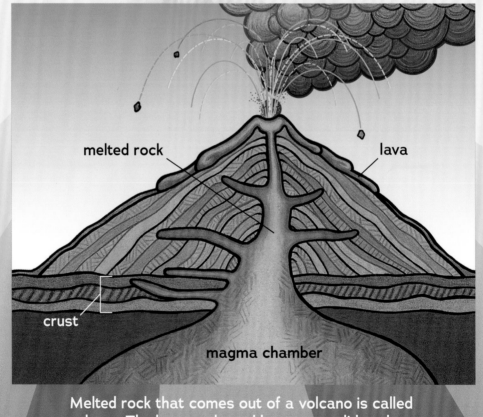

INSIDE A VOLCANO

melted rock

lava

crust

magma chamber

Melted rock that comes out of a volcano is called lava. The lava cools and becomes solid rock.

Lava

Sometimes the hot magma pushes all the way up to the surface. Then the volcano erupts. Melted rock comes out onto Earth's surface. Melted rock that comes out of a volcano is called lava.

Most volcanoes erupt for a while, and then they rest for a while. Over a long time, the cooled lava from a volcano can pile up to make a big mountain.

Some volcanoes erupt slowly. The magma begins to leak upward through the crust. When it gets to the surface, the magma becomes lava. The lava flows slowly across the ground, like a fiery river.

When a volcano erupts, hot lava might flow across the ground.

This volcano is spraying hot lava into the air.

Other volcanoes erupt very quickly. Under these volcanoes, magma pushes harder and harder against the sides of the magma chamber. Finally, it pushes so hard that the volcano explodes! Big, fiery globs of lava may fly through the air. These globs are called lava bombs. Gas and bits of rock come out of the ground too.

Chapter 4

MAKING NEW CRUST

The big, rocky plates of Earth's crust are always moving. They slide past one another. They crash together. Part of one plate may be pushed under another plate. When the edge of a plate is pushed down into the mantle, it melts. But that part of Earth's crust isn't gone forever.

When two of Earth's plates collide, the crust may wrinkle to form mountains. What else might happen when plates crash together?

Underwater Crust

The part of the crust that is under the oceans is very important. This is where new crust is made.

Some volcanoes form under the oceans. After a long time, an underwater volcano may grow tall enough to stick up above the water. Then it is called a volcanic island.

Under the oceans, the crust is thin. The mantle is close to the surface. In some places, the mantle pushes up along the cracks between the big plates. The plates bulge upward. These bulges become long ridges. Geologists call them mid-ocean ridges. Mid-ocean ridges are thousands of miles long. One big ridge is in the middle of the Atlantic Ocean. Another is under the Pacific Ocean.

HOW A VOLCANIC ISLAND GROWS

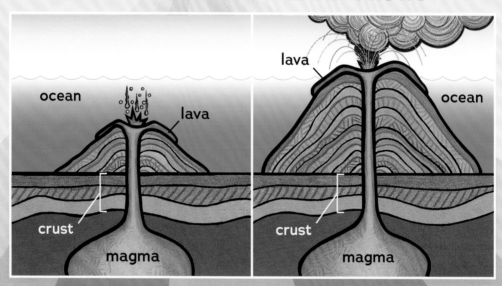

Lava piles up around an underwater volcano. The pile of lava slowly grows bigger and bigger. It becomes an underwater mountain. After a long time, the mountain sticks up above the water. It has become a volcanic island.

Rifts and Rock

Along the top of each ridge is a deep crack. The crack is called a rift. Magma slowly flows up through the rift. Lava pours out onto the ocean's bottom. The cold ocean water cools the lava, changing it into solid rock. This rock is new crust.

Old crust melts, and new crust forms. Earth's plates move and make mountains grow. Earth's crust is always changing.

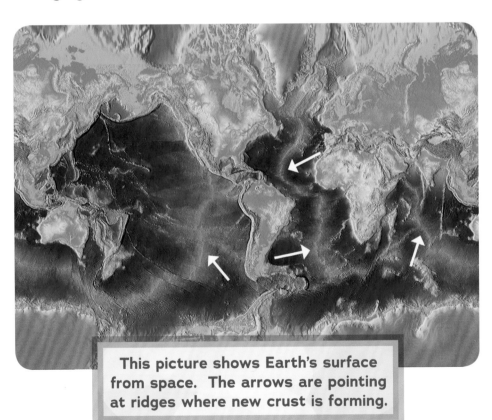

This picture shows Earth's surface from space. The arrows are pointing at ridges where new crust is forming.

Glossary

core: Earth's center. The core has two parts called the inner core and the outer core.

crust: Earth's rocky outer layer

earthquake: a movement of parts of Earth's crust that makes the ground shake

erupt: to let melted rock and gases go out onto Earth's surface

fault: a crack in Earth's crust

geologist: a scientist who studies Earth

lava: melted rock that comes out of a volcano

magma: melted rock inside Earth

magma chamber: a huge space under a volcano. The space is filled with hot melted rock.

mantle: the thick layer of rock under Earth's crust

mid-ocean ridge: a place under the ocean where pieces of Earth's crust bulge upward and new crust is formed

mountain: a big fold in Earth's crust

plate: a huge piece of Earth's crust

rift: a deep crack

volcano: a hole in Earth's crust

Learn More about Earth's Crust

Books

Fradin, Judith Bloom, and Dennis Fradin. *Volcano!: The Icelandic Eruption of 2010 and Other Hot, Smoky, Fierce, and Fiery Mountains*. Washington, DC: National Geographic, 2010. Learn about the intense happenings of volcanic eruptions and what else occurs when Earth's crust gets active.

Horobin, Wendy, and Caroline Stamps. *First Earth Encyclopedia*. New York: DK Publishing, 2010. Using maps and climate and weather information, this book introduces lots of fun facts about the world and its physical features.

Riley, Joelle. *Examining Erosion*. Minneapolis: Lerner Publications Company, 2013. Find out what erosion does to Earth's crust in this book about wind, water, and weathering.

Websites

Earth's Continental Plates
http://www.enchantedlearning.com/subjects/astronomy/planets/earth/Continents.shtml
This site includes animation that shows how the continents have moved during Earth's history.

Neighborhood Rocks
http://www.saltthesandbox.org/rocks/index.htm
Learn all about rock collecting! This website includes descriptions of some kinds of rocks you might find in your neighborhood.

OLogy: Plates on the Move
http://www.amnh.org/ology/features/plates
Interactive animations let you explore how Earth's plates affect our world.

Index

Photo Acknowledgments

The images in this book are used with the permission of: © Lori Andrews/Flickr/Getty Images, p. 4; © Fallsview/Dreamstime.com, p. 5; © James P. Rowan, pp. 6, 26; © Laura Westlund/Independent Picture Service, pp. 7, 15, 17, 21, 30, 36; NASA/JPL, p. 8; © Carsten Peter/National Geographic/CORBIS, p. 9; © Sam Lund/Independent Picture Service, p. 10; © Todd Strand/Independent Picture Service, p. 11; © Lcc54613/Dreamstime.com, p. 12; © Toshi Sasaki/Stone+/Getty Images, p. 13; © Jason Reed/Getty Images, p. 14; © Photodisc/Getty Images, p. 16; © Jason Hawkes/CORBIS, p. 18; © Nigel Pavitt/AWL Images/Getty Images, p. 19; © Tom Van Sant/GeoSphere/CORBIS, p. 20; © Jean-Pierre Pieuchot/Stone/Getty Images, p. 22; NASA/JSC, p. 23; © Martin Brown/Dreamstime.com, p. 24; © Galen Rowell/CORBIS, p. 25; © James Balog/Stone/Getty Images, p. 27; © Design Pics/Reyond Mainse/Perspectives/Getty Images, p. 28; © Doug Menuez/Photodisc/Getty Images, p. 29; © Andoni Canela/age fotostock/Getty Images, p. 31; © Digital Vision/Getty Images, p. 32; © iStockphoto.com/Pablo Hidalgo, p. 33; © Feng Wei Photography/Flickr/Getty Images, p. 34; © Amos Nachoum/CORBIS, p. 35; Courtesy of NOAA, p. 37. Front cover: © David Hogan/Flickr/Getty Images.

Main body text set in Adrianna Regular 14/20
Typeface provided by Chank